Bloom

A FLORAL COLORING BOOK FOR ADULTS

BY: KAREN SUE CHEN

Check out Sunshine-Creative.com for more products!
Share your work! #KarenSueStudios on social media.

Printed in the United States of America

First Printing, 2023

ISBN 978-1737007074
www.Sunshine-Creative.com

Dedicated to my
sister Jessica.

Check out Sunshine-Creative.com for more products!

A Note From the Author:

Thank you so much for purchasing Bloom! Your support allows me to pursue my dream of being a professional artist. I was born and raised in Texas, and I currently live in California. In my free time I enjoy gardening, yoga, acrobatics, crafting, roller skating, and hanging out with my pet dog.

If you enjoyed this book, check out my other coloring books Enchanted, Secret Worlds, Bite-Sized Worlds, Life of the Wild, Flora and Fauna, Mandala Daydream, Mandalas for Peace, Mandala Secret Garden, Soar, Gnome in the Home, and Magic Ocean at Sunshine-Creative.com.

It truly brings me joy to see your finished masterpieces! Please tag @KarenSueStudios or use #karensuestudios.

And always remember to let sunshine into your life!

Love,
Karen Sue Chen

f YouTube @KarenSueStudios

Share your work! #KarenSueStudios on social media.

love...

Check out Sunshine-Creative.com for more products!

“What is planted in each
person’s soul will sprout.”
-Rumi

Thank you for your support. You make it possible for me to pursue my dream as an artist. If you enjoyed this book, please leave a review on Amazon! Also, be sure to check out my other books at Sunshine-Creative.com.

Share your work! #KarenSueStudios on social media.

Made in the USA
Coppell, TX
18 February 2026

71661921R00046